WHAT YOUR DOG'S BREED SAYS ABOUT YOU

WHAT

YOUR

DOG'S BREED

SAYS ABOUT YOU

A FUN LOOK AT THE PECULIARITIES OF PETS AND THEIR OWNERS

JO HOARE

DOG 'n' BONE

Published in 2017 by Dog 'n' Bone Books
An imprint of Ryland Peters & Small Ltd
20–21 Jockey's Fields   341 E 116th St
London WC1R 4BW   New York, NY 10029

www.rylandpeters.com

10 9 8 7 6 5 4 3 2 1

A CIP catalog record for this book is available from the
Library of Congress and the British Library.

ISBN: 978 1 911026 12 9

Printed in China

Editor: Dawn Bates
Designer: Wide Open Studio
Illustrator: Steven Millington

CONTENTS

THE BREEDS

INTRODUCTION

Don't panic, this ISN'T a book about deciphering your dog's sighs, grunts, and barks. We're not going to tell you how every noise he makes is easily translatable into language. It's not literally "what your dog says about you," and, for the record, if he could speak the first thing he'd probably do was rat you out for all those years of blaming, what we'll delicately call, bodily functions on him. This won't be a how-to manual on understanding your mutt, because let's be honest you already get by perfectly on a language of tail wags, puppy-dog eyes, and furious sitting in the corner with back turned. Instead, it's a look at what your choice of dog really reveals about you—even if he chose you (yep, we all know when you went to pick your puppy, he was the one in charge, working his magic to ensure he'd be the one coming home with you).

We all know the stereotypes: there's the pampered princess and her diamond-collared Chihuahua in a Louis Vuitton case, and the hardman stalking the streets with his guard dog Staffie on a thick chain, but there's a lot more to take a closer look at. From your canine culinary choices to where you stand on pawdicures, the decisions you make about your pup's life reveal a lot about you.

So we recommend you flick straight to your breed, find out exactly how true it is to you (admit it, it is), then spend some time looking up the breeds that belong to people you know (I'd put money on the fact you choose the people you don't really like first. See page 62 for your annoying sister-in-law's pug). And if you don't yet have a pooch (WHY THE HELL NOT?), then maybe this book will help make the choice for you...

THE ISSUES

EAU DE DOGS

No matter how clean you try to keep your pup, there are always going to be times when she is more than a little stinky. Non-dog lovers can sniff out even the slightest hint of canine odor with all the ferocity of a bloodhound (they wouldn't thank you for that comparison) and, although it's tough to admit, us dog owners are at times a little guilty of smell blindness. How many of these are familiar to you?

FOX POOP

What is it about this particular animal expulsion that dogs love? Sure, they can be pretty partial to other types of poop too—they'll take what they can find—but fox poop is like a beautiful, rare elixir that they cannot help but coat themselves in. To a dog it might be Chanel No. 5, but to you and everyone else who comes into close proximity with anything your dog has come into contact with (have you ever smelt a car that's transported a fox-poop roller?), it's tantamount to poison gas.

Experts say the compulsion for a dog to cover itself in c*** is handed down from its ancestors, who would have had to smell like their environment when hunting down prey to eat. Well, their environment is now a quilted bed and they get three meals a day so quit it, okay?

PRODUCTS

Now, your use of doggy shampoos and soaps might actually be what's driving your pup to coat himself in poop. Dogs hate to smell fresh and flowery, so if it's a choice between a few days' freshness followed by an avalanche of dirty-puddle rolling or a low-level natural doggy stink, we'd go for the latter every time. Pet perfumes and colognes promise to leave your dog smelling of anything from baby powder to freshly baked apple

pie. When we say promise...
imagine a hint of synthetic
fragrance mixed with doggy
smells and it's not a winning
combo. Best leave them natural.

DOG BREATH

This is an insult for a reason.
Dogs can have absolutely terrible
halitosis. So would you if you
didn't brush your teeth. Try mint
chews, dog-friendly toothpaste,
or just staying at least arm's
length away at all times...

FLATULENCE

There's very little you can do
about your dog's gaseous
emissions, so just embrace
the fact that you've always
got someone else to blame
your own on.

DOG BUTT COVERS

We couldn't complete this
entry without talking about
these. Yes, they're actually
a thing. These stickers
(designs include a cupcake,
a pair of dice, and a sheriff's
badge) are designed to
stop other dogs invading
your pup's private
passageway with
their nosey snouts,
and also to keep
them "fresh and
clean" around your
soft furnishings...
I'd stay well away.

UPSTAIRS, DOWNSTAIRS

No greater question divides dog owners than whether or not they're the type of person who allows their dog on the furniture. Does their pet have free reign over the sofas and armchairs and scamper upstairs to bed alongside them or is he strictly relegated to his own bed downstairs? Neither party understands the other—the one who thinks furniture is strictly for humans recoils at the thought of dog hair all over their finest soft furnishings. Their dog would no more climb up the stairs than drive the family car. The one who lets the dog sit wherever they do, thinks the furniture denier to be a cruel breed and cannot imagine a night not snuggled close to their four-legged friend. If you're the latter, bear these dos and don'ts in mind:

DOS AND DON'TS

DO think about how much your pup disturbs your sleep. If he snores, moves frequently, or is just too damn big, he'll disrupt your sleep. You might not even be aware of it until you wonder why you're so tired every morning.

DO think about your sex life, especially if you have a new partner. Dogs can get VERY jealous of new bedmates...

DO remember that once you've let your dog up on the sofa/in the bed, it will be very difficult to stop him. You may start with a cute hand-sized puppy snuggled up on your lap or curled up at the foot of your bed, but fast forward a year or two and you're bed- or sofa-sharing with a pooch that weighs almost the same as you.

DO try to teach your dog an "off" command, so if you have visitors that don't appreciate sharing their chair/pillow/dreams with your beloved pal, they have the option not to.

DO get a vacuum cleaner with a pet hair attachment if your dog sheds. Nobody wants to look like they've sat in a tumbleweed every time they watch TV. Some non-pet-friendly vacuums have the unwanted ability to spread a dog's scent as it "cleans," spraying stench around the house. Who wants a room stinking unnecessarily of dog?

DON'T let an already dominant dog on the furniture—he'll definitely think he's the boss.

DON'T let your dog sleep in your bed if you have allergies or asthma. Night-time will give you some time to breathe "clean" air.

DOG SOCIAL MEDIA

Everyone knows that friend who simply will not shut up about her baby on social media, from details of the birth (vomit) to weekly, daily, hourly, minute-ly (not a word we know but it needs to be, if only for use in this situation) pictoral updates of the infant doing various cute things. By "cute things" we mean just laying there, because that's all the poor kid can do—it's a baby. And the worst crime of all? The ever-popular "humorous" diaper share. Hint: no one needs to see another human's waste products on social media, even if that human is the most precious gem to grace this earth (it's not). Anyway, we digress; back to the far more important business of dogs and social media. Should you and, if so, what are your options?

HOW MUCH IS TOO MUCH?

Your dog is ridiculously photogenic, and no it's not just you that thinks that—you got 15 likes last time you uploaded a photo of her wearing a crown at Christmas/comedy sunglasses/ a jaunty hat, so you know you're not alone in your adoration. Surely the next step then is to give her a social media profile? But which one? And does she have her own voice or do "Mama" and "Daddy" speak for her? Which hashtags are best? Should you invest in a tag that collects her activity and feeds it directly to her account— a kind of canine Fitbit, if you will. A collar-mounted GoPro? Oh it's a minefield.

THE OPTIONS

DOGBOOK: This Facebook-esque site was the first online community to realize that dogs need to know about the minutiae of their pals' lives too. Impressively, it now has three million users. It's probably better written than 97 percent of the posts you see on your regular Facebook—even if the dogs are typing with their paws.

DOGNAMIC.COM: This social media website has a Grindr-esque feature so you can see who the "hot" dogs are near you. If that's your thing.

DOGSTER.COM: More of an info website with community aspects. Ask your dog her opinion of this one—she might not feel it's interactive enough.

TO SHAME OR NOT TO SHAME?

So your beloved has just been a right little horror and eaten a packet of crayons (hello rainbow poop)/humped a visiting child/peed all over a fresh bundle of laundry. Do you:

a. Huff and puff and go through your entire back catalog of swear words before dealing with the situation?

b. Decide to share his crime with the world and "dog shame" him?

This involves taking a picture of your guilty-looking pup in front of the aforementioned crayons/slightly ruffled baby/pee-drenched clothes and sharing it with the world. Fun, right? Well, animal welfare experts say it could be undermining his dignity. So if you're gonna do it, best up the parental controls on his Internet access...

THE VIRAL SUCCESSES

Want to make your dog go viral so she can pay for her own vaccinations and poop bags? For inspiration here are a few of the most-viewed pooches on YouTube.

SPIDER DOG
A popular choice around Halloween, this involves putting a spider costume on your pup and, once it gets dark, letting him run up and "scare" people. Chica, the original spider dog has had 165 million views. And terrified a LOT of people.

FENTON
The posh British man who screams at his deer-chasing dog in London's Richmond Park was one of the biggest viral hits of 2011. Maybe not the best one to copy, dashing after livestock can get you into a lot of hot water.

THE GUITAR LOVING RETRIEVER
There's lots of chat about whether or not this is a beer commercial, but whatever... it's SO cute! As his owner strums the guitar, the Goldie smiles and nods his head in time to the music. Whenever the owner stops playing, the dog stops moving his head and ditches the smile. Addictive viewing.

ULTIMATE DOG TEASE
This famous viral dog video, racking up over 185 million views, shows an owner telling his dog the ultimate tale of the delicious treats he has in the fridge while the dog seemingly talks along.

THE FAN OF ADELE'S *HELLO*
A relative newcomer, this cute little fluffy ball is camouflaged as he lays on a white fluffy blanket, before popping his head up, perfectly in time to Adele's opening "Hello."

THE HOBBIES

Yes, you read that right, like the perma-exhausted pre-schooler ferried from "Mandarin for Toddlers" to "Fencing for Under-Fives," your dog's downtime is scarce. And don't think you can count hiding socks under the kitchen table or rolling on his back in fox poop as "hobbies." Sure, he might enjoy these things but everyone knows "enjoyment" is pretty low down on the list of reasons to do hobbies. If it was really all about pleasure then everyone's hobby would just be laying down wondering whether to eat a cookie or have a nap. And then what would they put on their dating profiles? Today's dog needs a busy schedule to feel truly fulfilled. Here are a few activities to keep him out of trouble...

DOG YOGA OR DOGA

Now you're going to have to get off your butt for this too. It's actually a "partner" hobby, meaning you've got to join your dog in the, erm, downward dog position.

Some dogs are already practicing this without your knowledge, and if you've got a dog on your hands that likes stretching, wiggling his butt, or kicking out his back legs after a snooze then according to doga experts (yes, that is an actual thing) he's a natural and well on the path to becoming a full-on yogi (dogi?).

What you're aiming for is a "sense of energy and flow" between dog and owner. And, no, you can't get that by both sitting in a car with your heads out of the window... Should your pup be sturdy enough, he may be the one supporting you in poses (maybe don't try this if he's a Chihuahua and you're still carrying a little vacation weight) or you can gently manipulate him. Doga fans report the only downside is a yoga mat that is almost entirely coated in drool. Ewww.

DOG PAINTING

Paw-casso? Vincent van Dog? Bark Rothko? (Okay, getting a bit desperate now.) There could be a supremely talented artist side-eyeing you from under the table right now. And with some dog artists commanding as much as $1,700 a painting, your pup could definitely be earning his keep. Worried he'll struggle to hold the brush? There are a few options...

1. THE BOWL PUSH
Dogs at London's Battersea Dogs Home have created their masterpieces with oil pastels attached to their food bowls— as they push the bowl around, it creates patterns.

2. THE PAW PRINTS
Like the countless baby footprints you've doubtlessly received over the years (tip: if you don't want one, don't buy Christening gifts), you can cover your pooch's paws with color and then let him run over your canvas. Make sure your paints are safe—those in the know say cornstarch, water, and food coloring are best. Just make sure you hose him off before he goes near your cream carpet.

3. TOOTH BRUSH
Yep, some mutts are genuinely clever enough to work out how to hold the brush between their teeth and put paint to canvas. An ex-service dog called Sammy became so skilled at this that he made a fortune selling his work. It's unlikely your pet will reach quite the same heights as Sammy, but why not have a go and see if you can unleash your dog's inner Degas? Remember, though, if you want to indulge your dog's creative streak just make sure the paints you choose are safe for him to swallow.

DOG SINGING

Reckon you've got an alto Alsatian on your hands? Maybe a Springer soprano? Fancy bringing on tinnitus and a three-day migraine? Why not enrol your mutt in a canine choir? Yes, it's JUST as bad as it sounds.

DOG SURFING

With a whole competition devoted to it in California, dog surfing is big business, and it's been around a lot longer than you might think. Surfing dogs were first seen on the beaches of California and Hawaii in the 1920s, and now there's a whole industry around it. Experts recommend starting your dog off out of the water, and feeding him his meals on the board to get him used to it, then building up to getting him to perform commands on the board, before introducing him to a life-jacket and then bringing the whole lot together. Probably not one to try if your pooch gave up at "Sit"...

DOGS AND DATING

Now if you've come to this looking for dogging advice, we're afraid you're literally barking up the wrong tree. Might we suggest a quick Google search instead. But definitely not on your work computer and probably best to delete your history at home... Now that's out of the way, we'll move on to what we really mean. How to exploit the fact you have a dog to get you dates. Yay!

ONLINE DATING

A profile picture with a cute dog, or even one that's not cute but has that ugly-cute thing going on, instantly adds two points onto everyone's average. Think you're a six? Add a selfie with a grinning Golden Retriever and you're instantly an eight. Worried you're only a five? Cradling a puppy, any puppy, and it'll take you right up to a seven—steal one for five seconds in the street if necessary (but maybe ask first)—further down the line, you can always pretend it got run over/your cruel ex took it and, bang, you've elicited even more sympathy. And if you see someone you like and their profile pic has a dog in it, ALWAYS make your first message about the dog—it'll increase your chances of a reply by around 347 percent.

IRL DATING

In this day and age, if you talk to a stranger in the street people tend to presume you're either a) crazy; b) trying to sell them something; c) crazy and trying to sell them something. If you've both got a dog, however, you've already got a bigger icebreaker than the Titanic with which to start a conversation.

Here are some dos and don'ts:

DO begin with a compliment that's also a question to warm up the object of your affections. "What a beautiful coat your dog has. I've never seen one quite that color before. Is it a very rare type?" Perhaps it's best not to try this technique on someone walking a black Labrador, but you get the idea.

DO stick to walking the same route at the same time each day if you happen to see someone you like. Dogs and their owners are creatures of habit, so if you first see that fit, sporty type doing an early-morning jog with his Spaniel in the park, he'll probably be there a few mornings a week. One or two days of eye contact and you'll quickly progress to saying hello and from there who knows..

DON'T lurk in the bushes waiting for your crush to walk past so you can accidentally bump into him or her. You'll look like you're dogging (see opposite) or peeing.

DON'T attempt to initiate conversation while either of you are engaged in poop scooping. Do we need to tell you why?

NAMES

What's in a name? Well, quite a lot actually. Remember you're going to be shrieking it at the top of your voice for the rest of your dog's life. Which route have you gone down?

PEDIGREE NAMES

With a complicated equation of breeder, ancestor, and plain old-fashioned whimsy, pedigree pups' names tend to sound like the children of 19th-century aristocrats who were doped up on laudanum when it came to registering their children's names. Don't believe us? These are the genuine names of former Crufts competitors.

• Lochtaymor Bridget Jones of Tillycorthie
• Dyrham Playboy of Chilworth
• Plumhollow Top Hat
• Chartan Luna Lovegood of Dubhagusdonn
• Cheveralla Ben of Banchory
• Hendrawen's Nibelung of Charavigne
• Oakington Puckshill Amber Sunblush

Get your own by taking the name of your school, followed by your mother's/father's (appropriate to the gender of your dog) name and finally the first object you see if you turn to your left—Marlborough Beverley of Purple Cushion if you're asking...

CAUSE CELEBRE NAMES

Reality TV show winners, trophy-winning sportsmen, favorite soap stars—the problem with this category is that with fame today being more fleeting than your average case of tonsillitis, naming your dog after whoever's just scored a goal/married a movie star does date rather rapidly. Plus everyone else has the same idea, so it's like shouting Britney into a class of early 2000s' school kids.

SAME DIFFERENCE

Beloved of the more practical of the dog owners, this somewhat Royalistic approach to naming means giving every dog you ever have exactly the same name. Largely now an archaic practice, existing only in pockets of particularly posh parts of Britain, it saves on dog tags and owner's head space.

REGRET 'EM NAMES

This is a painful category. You let your ex name your pup, and it was so romantic. Cooing and cuddling over little baby Poochie-Woochie, love blinding you to the fact that it's really bloody embarrassing shouting that in a busy park. Then the bitch (not the dog variety) broke your heart and ran off with Mark from work, leaving Poochie-Woochie and her wardrobe of diamanté collars as the only memory of your lost love. Poochie has got you through it, though, and to be honest the dog is a better bedfellow than your ex, but every time you call her name it's a dagger to your heart. You've tried to rename her, but she's stubborn and refuses to answer to anything else, leaving you both humiliated and desolate every time she runs off on a walk...

FOOD

There's a lot more to feeding your dog than just spooning out some chunks of canned dog food twice a day. And what you choose to nourish your pooch says a hell of a lot about you. Which of these is your dog?

ORGANIC DOGS

You are rich. You probably claim to have at least one food intolerance—it has never been diagnosed by a doctor, but you took a survey in *Women's Health* which, in your opinion, is actually to be trusted more than global medicine, which is by and large a conspiracy. Your dog has a team of "people" involved in its life—swimming coaches, canine therapist, grooming "artist," and a busier calendar than the child of a Tiger mom.

VEGAN DOGS

You've got a lot of time on your hands. You've experimented with making your own dog food. You pay more for your dog food than you do your own. Your dog takes more supplements than a bodybuilder. Your dog sneaks roadkill when out of sight and your friends feed him titbits when you're not looking. You've definitely visited a holistic vet and you're sure the $300 non-toxic flea powder he sold you will start working any day now. Until then, well, he also sold you something for the bites you keep getting. That was only $150 and it's definitely making a bit of difference to the itching...

SUPERMARKET DOGS

You buy what's on offer. In bulk. You take it home. Your dog eats it. You are normal. Your dog cannot tell the difference between brands because he is a dog and cannot read the labels. His bowl is an old one you once used for cereal.

COOKED FOR EVERY NIGHT DOGS

Your dog is the boss of you. Everyone you know thinks you are ridiculous. You have an array of fine china for him to eat from and his bowls sit upon a mat that has his initials monogrammed on it. You definitely call yourself Mommy and Daddy. When other people look after your dog it gets food from a can and eats every last bit.

TREATS FROM THE TABLE DOGS

Your dog is fat. People who come to your house for dinner get annoyed by his begging, but don't say anything. They then moan about you behind your back, but it saves you having to invite them again.

POOP-TIQUETTE:
THE POLITICS OF POOP

Put simply, what goes in has to come out and EVERY dog owner has to deal with this in some way. Even if you're a literal Lord of the Manor with acres and acres of land and a full-time professional poop picker-upper, there's definitely still been that incident on a family member's carpet/stranger's lawn/busy street with hundreds of people tutting at you. How you deal with what we'll euphemistically call your dogs "outgoings" says a lot about you as an owner. Recognize yourself here?

THE NO NONSENSE

You always have a ready supply of bags—never less than four, two for you (well your dog, or this is something else entirely), one for emergencies, and one extra to dole out to forgetful types using their lack of bag as an excuse to get out of poop scooping (more on them to come). You've tried and tested many types, bar the scented ones, which you consider as ridiculous frippery, and settled on what you believe to be the correct ratio of thickness/ease of tying and value. You buy them quarterly in bulk. You can sniff out your dog's business at ten paces and have developed the perfect technique of hand in bag, pick up, and tie all in seconds, no matter what confronts you. Woe betide those who don't meet your high poop disposal standards as you don't think they should be allowed to have dogs at all...

THE PANICKER

You live in constant fear of being caught without a bag and, as such, every pocket/glove box/bag contains at least one scrunched-up poop bag that's probably been there so long that, like that out-of-date condom at the back of your medicine cabinet, it definitely isn't fit for purpose. You're never quite sure how many bags you need for a walk and still haven't worked out an approximate routine for your dog's ablutions, so live in constant fear of her squatting when you're under-prepared. This probably harks back to childhood and getting caught out and publicly shamed for being minus a bag. Maybe consider therapy.

THE "MAKE HIM DO SOME OF THE WORK"

You are fed up of lugging round handfuls of scrunched-up plastic, so have invested in a little coat or collar that comes with pockets for your dog to carry her own bags. A great idea apart from if your dog is a "poop-and-run" type, in which case it's a mad dash to get the bag, then ten minutes looking for it in the manner of a particularly revolting "X marks the spot" treasure map.

THE HANGMAN

One of the great mysteries of the dog-owning world is who the hell are the people who insist on hanging bags of poop from tree branches and park railings? Why go through all the horrid bit of

actually scooping, but then give up on the final hurdle of walking a few steps to a bin? Instead they display the poop bag artistically, like hanging fruit, from the nearest tree where it becomes the most horrendous peril for anyone of a certain height. Confront "The Hangman" and he'll claim he'll pick it up at the end of his walk. Yeah right...

THE OUT AND OUT IGNORER

This owner has a terribly rare ocular condition known as SPRB, or Selective Poop-Related Blindness. As soon as his dog starts hinting that some business might

be about to occur—circular walking, extra sniffing, glancing over his shoulder to see who's watching—he is suddenly rendered entirely sightless to any field of vision his dog appears in. He will be suddenly fixated straight ahead, his eyes glassy and unseeing until mercifully his dog finishes. Science has yet to find a cure for this cruel affliction.

THE "I FORGOT BAGS"

If you're an oopser, then may we congratulate you on your acting abilities. That mime you do when hovering over what we know is probably a hideous mess, of patting yourself down with airline security precision as if there might just be a bag concealed upon your person that you're unaware of, the theatrical turning out of empty pockets, the caricature-like grimace of cursing your own

forgetfulness...IT AIN'T FOOLING NO ONE. Best way to deal with this is to rush over and offer one of your own. Preferably the one at the bottom of your bag that you know your keys have poked a hole in.

THE "OOPS I REALLY DID FORGET THE BAGS"

There's no panic like the genuine no-bag panic, and your dog is somehow psychically attuned to know the rare occasions that this happens and goes out of her way to produce the greatest need for one you ever had. You have a number of options when this happens:

1. RUN as fast as you can. Do not turn around. Do not stop to collect your belongings. Just get out of there.

2. RELY ON NATURE but this gruesome choice should only be done in extreme desperation i.e. your pooch has just gone on the grassy lawn of a village fete or church social in front of everyone you've ever known. You attempt to fashion some kind of rudimentary shovel from a selection of leaves and twigs. It won't be pretty, but at least you'll look like you've made the effort.

3. BEG someone around you for a spare poop bag. Do you have anything you could barter with them? A cigarette, some chocolate, your husband?

THE WORLD'S WORST DOG POOP STORY

As a PS to this and to make you feel better about your own poop horror stories, spare a thought for the poor couple who woke up to find their entire house looking like it was starring in a scatological remake of *Carrie*.

Owners of dogs and a Roomba robot vacuum cleaner (it's a circular flat disc that you program to come on and vacuum your house while you are out or asleep etc) take note now. This couple's puppy pooped on a rug in the middle of the night, just before the Roomba was programmed to start. The Roomba then skated over the poop and coated every single floor surface (and some walls... one word: splashback) with the results of the poor pup's rather poorly tummy. The couple woke up to a crying toddler absolutely coated in unpleasantness and it took days of cleaning. Best stick to a Dyson, hey...

DOG GROOMING

From a monthly once-over with an old hairbrush to a two-day spa visit to The Paw Seasons or Chateau Marmutt (these are real destinations—look them up if you don't believe me), there's a huge spectrum of pooch pampering. Find out where you stand on four-legged friend grooming with our quiz.

1. How many brushes do you own specifically for your dog?

   a. Hmmmm, when you say specifically does it matter if it's occasionally used on the kids when you're in a hurry to get out of the door?

   b. A couple. You were convinced to try a Furminator by persistent marketing emails from a pet food company you once ordered some organic dog breath freshener from.

   c. You're not sure, you'd have to unpack your special grooming wheelie case.

2. What's your preferred doggy drying routine?

   a. You will wipe him down with an old towel you ruined with hair dye if he's really soaking wet.

   b. You've tried to give him a once-over with the hairdryer, but poor Fluffy is petrified of the noise.

   c. A full blow-dry. How else would you get the perfect finish on his new color rinse?

3. We say pawdicure, you say...

   a. What?

   b. You're not on board with the cutesy name but you get his claws trimmed as and when.

   c. This Thursday. But you prefer the term mutt-icure.

4. Extreme grooming is…

a. The reason you have parental filters on your Internet connection.
b. Pretty stupid. Why do you want your dog dyed and dried to look like a panda or tiger?
c. Your raison d'être.

5. How many of the following have you treated your pooch to? (These are all real things people pay money for. Madness.)

- Mud treatment
- Skin analysis
- Tear stain cleanse
- Whitening treatment
- Ear massage
- Ozone spa bath

a. None of them. And you have no idea what most of them mean.
b. Goldie may have been given a quick whitening freshen up.
c. All of them; every week.

MOSTLY As
You love your mutt, but how he looks (or smells) isn't that important. Just watch out if guests start bringing their own air freshener.

MOSTLY Bs
You seem to be at a sensible level of grooming. Stay away from the wacky stands at pet shows and you should be okay.

MOSTLY Cs
You might want to have a little word with yourself before your canine beauty therapist talks you into doggy hair extensions…

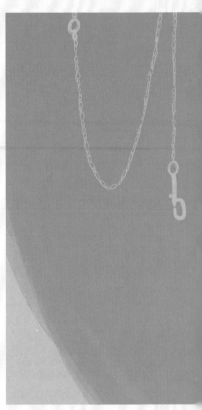

THE
BREEDS

THE GOLDEN RETRIEVER

Shaggy, blond, at times a little smelly but loyal and oh so lovably dim, the Golden Retriever owner... just kidding... The Golden Retriever elicits feelings of love in even those strange people who claim not to like dogs. Walking a Golden Retriever puppy down the street brings about levels of attention comparable to having J-Lo in a diamanté thong on the end of a leash. Even as Retrievers get older (and yes, smellier) people still cross the road to give them a cuddle.

The Goldie's puppy-dog eyes are its number one weapon. No matter how severe the roll in fox poop (it's Chanel No. 5 to a GR), how bad the wind in the back seat on a long car journey, how much of the dinner left on the kitchen counter is scoffed before you notice, it's impossible to tell Retrievers off without feeling like the meanest person in the world when they settle those remorseful chocolate brown peepers on you. That's not to say this is the only weapon in the Goldie's emotional arsenal—they are also blessed with one hell of a smile. Look at any happy Golden Retriever and she'll be grinning. It's no surprise really as she's probably got three different beds at home (all with higher thread counts than the family's Egyptian cotton bed sheets), her own chair in the living room (covered in blankets obviously, for the GR owner appreciates not every guest might want to come away with what looks like Donald Trump attached to their backside), and a personalized water bowl she "unwrapped" on Christmas morning. Not that you'll see any of this paraphernalia of pamperedness should you visit (well, not if you're an important guest), for GR owners like to maintain a veneer of strictness, pretending that they are very much the masters, with the dog firmly knowing her place in the family. That the Goldie certainly does— she's number one by a country mile.

A Golden Retriever does have to work hard for her comforts, though. The disadvantage of being the most photogenic of breeds is that EVERYONE wants to take her picture and it's hard work being beautiful all the time. The Goldie's cuteness factor also means every toddler will mistake the dog for a soft toy and hang themselves from the animal's neck as the patient pooch plods around the living room, wishing they'd all just clear off so she can have a nap in peace.

The only downside to Goldies, as any owner will know, is their adoration of mud given how difficult it is to clean them up. Like a water-divining

expert, the Goldie will find the only patch of grime in an otherwise dry-as-a-bone field and immediately plunge herself headlong into it, resulting in a mud tide line up to the haunches and a half blond, half murky greeny-brown pooch.

Goldies adore water, whether it's a smelly river full of duck poop (sorry for the repeated fecal mentions, but they really do love it) or a filthy puddle they can lay in on their backs, like Homer Simpson on a lilo in the pool. But try to get them anywhere near something scented and clean and they are out of there. These cleaning attempts usually result in a tussle in the garden that require at least three people— one to hold the hose, one to hold the dog, and one to fetch the freshly warmed towel in which to wrap and cuddle the dog after its traumatic experience.

THE FRENCH BULLDOG

There was a time when to know whether an area was specifically gay-friendly you looked for a rainbow flag—now you look for these grumpy little things, French Bulldogs. Expensive, fussy, and oh-so-photogenic, when it comes to social media the FB is the #avocadoontoast of the canine world. The perfect combination of tough and cute—just like his owners, newly-weds Marcus and Nathan. He's their fur baby and his haircut definitely costs more than yours. They would have gone for a Pug, but with every woman and her dog (literally) having one and their snub-nosed faces being emblazoned on more cheap T-shirts than Pooma, Nick, and Adides, they're far too basic for such sophisticates.

The Frenchie was once known as a "whore's dog" for its popularity amongst Parisian streetwalkers, and it may be that as a result of these experiences, of seeing all and sundry do all and sundry to his mistress, the FB has a glum little face. His grumpy little chops are at odds with his comical temperament and providing things are going his way—not too hot, no kids around, the only dog in a specific radius, the whole sofa to himself, no loud noises, personal chef, 800-thread count sheets—he's generally amiable enough.

One thing Marcus and Nathan weren't expecting, though, was just how stinky little Beau/Pierre/Etienne was going to be, for no amount of organic fresh mint dental chews can combat the breath of a creature who snuffles and snorts all day.

The flatulence is equally bad, but due to the amount of time Marcus and Nathan spend around men who only consume red meat and protein shakes, they're largely immune to that.

The Frenchie is smart but tricky to train as he already knows he's the boss, plus his comical facial expressions make it very difficult to tell him off. His one true motivation in life is the promise of food, but as it's oh so easy for him to cross from chunk to chub, and he really only likes to walk from sofa to bed and back again, an eye must be kept on his diet and exercise. One type of workout the FB must definitely avoid is swimming as due to his, ahem, sturdier frame, he will most likely sink. A lesson a panicked Marcus won't forget in a hurry (and nor will his pair of limited edition suede Gucci mule loafers).

THE BOXER

Boxer owners may have thought they were getting a guard dog, and the stance, bark, and speed of this breed would seem to support this, but there's one fatal flaw (that also happens to be the thing their owners love best)—their absolute soppiness. Oh yes, they may look fierce but a Boxer's biggest personality trait is thinking she is a human and that leads to far more silliness than scariness. The boxer seems largely unaware she is a dog—a fact most owners are happy to go along with because sitting upright at the breakfast table and traveling in the front seat of the car do make for very amusing photographs. Maybe it's the fault of those prints that appeared in bars in the '80s showing Boxers smoking, shooting pool, and playing cards. Perhaps popping out with the master for a bag of pork crackling and a beer and spotting these works of art made previous generations of Boxers fully aware of their position in the household?

The Boxer lives a life of two halves, so rules the house in two very different ways depending on her age. As a puppy she will be rambunctious, crazy, and bouncy, demanding an exercise regime that'd make Lance Armstrong need a lie down. This will be when the owners fool themselves into thinking that despite this boundless energy, they can be the boss of their Boxer.

When they're still small enough to be taken in the desired direction of whoever's on the other end of the leash, you'll convince yourself that you've cracked this dog training thing. Your Boxer isn't going to beat you, place laid at the table or not. You're still really in charge... 50-odd pounds (25 kilograms) of muscle later and it's a very different story...

As Boxers enter middle age, regardless of sex, they take on the curmudgeonly fancies of an upper crust Englishman enjoying an afternoon in a gentleman's club (and their gaseous outputs aren't dissimilar to someone who's enjoyed a light lunch of foie gras, peppered fillet steak, and half a bottle of cognac whilst dining at this aforementioned club), sulking at any slight change in their routine, detesting the heat, and slobbering on anything and anyone that gets in their way.

When the Boxer reaches this point, the owner chooses to go one of two ways. The first option is to become a desperate apologist for their haughty statesman of a pet, anticipating each misdemeanor well in advance and coming up with ever more creative ways to say sorry for the grumpiness/stubbornness/gassiness of their pet. Option two, and this is what most people do, is to embrace the curmudgeonly behavior fully, and begin to take on some of the traits themselves. After all, who's going to argue with someone with an enormous Boxer by their side?

THE COCKER SPANIEL

Are you frequently misplacing things you've put down? Was the last time you had a matching pair of socks five years ago? Do you keep your shoes at waist height or above at all times? Sounds like you're a Cocker Spaniel owner. The treasure hunters of the dog world, maybe it's a throwback to their working dog days, maybe they just think they're helping you keep things safe—whatever the reason, the Cocker is a total klepto, and nothing is safe.

Typically he'll have a hiding place for his treasures—and he definitely considers them treasures. He will never damage the rare jewels of holey socks, underwear from the laundry basket, and discarded children's soft toys, using his soft mouth to transport his spoils safely. This means your missing items will be intact, but probably so slobbery they can never be salvaged (ever tried putting a leather brogue in the wash? A Cocker owner has and it doesn't end well).

The hiding place may be under the dining room table, or behind the curtains or the shed—wherever your pup thinks his treasures are least likely to be disturbed. He'll then guard these precious finds with the pride of a lioness safeguarding her cubs. Occasionally, and often if there's a visitor around, he may permit a viewing of his collection, presenting his hoard in a carefully choreographed presentation on the lawn or, if the visitor is really in his good books, he or she may be presented with a gift of an old shoe on arrival. (temporary, of course, as it must be returned on leaving).

Cocker owners must always be prepared to have any part of their body used as a chair. From lap to shoulder to head. Sit still for more than a few minutes and a fluffy bum will perch itself precariously. This makes for a most handy scarf during the winter months, so nobody minds really.

When he's not hunting for treasure or using his owner as a sofa, the Cocker closely resembles an enthusiastic drunk, clumsily crashing into tables and chairs and tumbling hard in attempts to scale the dizzy heights of the sofa. He haphazardly bounds around until his energy finally gives out and just like the

aftermath of a six-pint night, he crashes out, flat on his back, legs splayed, manhood and belly on show for everyone. This kind of oblivious, dead-to-the-world sleep is but an unheard-of luxury to his owner, though, as the Cocker is also a highly effective alarm clock, timing his morning leap onto his master's bed with precision. It usually comes at the moment of deepest slumber and on the part of the body that'll shock them the most. You could, of course, shut your Cocker out of your bedroom, but then he'll have the whole house to ransack for his treasures... It's a lose-lose situation.

THE SPRINGER SPANIEL

A Springer Spaniel owner will be extremely fit or extremely exhausted. Because this pooch possesses energy reserves that were she an athlete would lead to her being banned. A Springer doesn't need illegal substances—she gets by on pure joy. Joy that results in her almost knocking you to the ground when you return home; or when you say the W.A.L.K word (I'm spelling it out in case you're reading aloud and she's in the vicinity); or when she hears her food cupboard being opened and... you get the picture. A whole lot of joy. A whole lot of struggling to stay upright.

It is wise not to leave a Springer Spaniel alone. With her quite frankly hydraulic limbs she lives up to her name. Unlike the lazy Retriever who looks at you with disdain and an expression that says "Retrieve? Well it's mine now, you threw it away" every time you try to coax him into retrieving a ball/Frisbee/$40 educational tool that the lady in the shop promised would teach him to fetch. Or the unaptly named West Highland terrier that's never even been to Scotland. Yes, the Springer is Springy. That means NOTHING is safe—closed doors are no match for her bouncing against the handle, baby stairgates are cleared in Olympic fashion, and that really, really high shelf—well that's just a hop, skip, and a sofa bounce to reach.

She will want to follow you anywhere and everywhere, so if you want to have a bath in peace without your pooch jumping headfirst into the square inch of free space she can see, then it's wise to invest in a lock.

Affectionate but never needy, the Springer loves you deeply but has no time to sit still and be petted for more than a few minutes—she needs to be busy. And that means as her owner, you do too. You will soon develop reactions nearly, but not quite as fast as hers—that dash after next-door's rabbit/child/mailman will always leave you floundering.

Oh, and every Springer owner knows to never be too far away from a towel. From the pile next to the door to the emergency threadbare ones in the car, life with a Springer means water. And lots of it. From deep diving into the grottiest of rivers to finding an inch of fetid puddle, if it's wet and grubby she will be into it. Headfirst and shaking it all over anyone foolish enough to come near.

A Springer owner is unlikely to be one of those shoes off/ all drinks on a coaster/leave the loo seat down type bores. It will always be a fun night round theirs...

THE COCKAPOO

Now the Kennel Club might refuse to acknowledge any kind of hybrid cross as a "proper" breed, but what do they know? The Cockapoo or Cockerpoo (and in some countries they're even called Spoodles, which is gorgeously ridiculous but adds to the confusion) might divide owners, but the one thing everyone who meets one agrees on is that these curly bundles of energy will steal your heart (and your socks, but more on that later).

With more bounce than a rough day at sea on Leonardo DiCaprio's yacht (think supermodels in unsupportive bikinis), the Cockapoo has some kind of trampoline-esque hydraulics sequestered in his hind legs. This means that all those high surfaces you thought it was safe to leave your dinner/socks/important papers on soon result in "hunger" followed closely by a $200 trip to the vet to get him to bring up the sock ('cos it'll get wrapped round his intestine, not because you have an unnatural attachment to your hosiery) or having to tell the boss your dog ate your homework, even though you're 45 and a neurology consultant. This Tigger-like ability is also interesting with toddlers— a Cockapoo can take out a roomful with one bounce— and men of a certain height, who would be advised to wear a protective sports cup should they be planning on owning this breed and remaining fertile. Cockapoo owners are forever apologizing for their dog bouncing into people, but secretly take pride in it, especially when it's the little brat belonging to your partner's friend who you've never liked being knocked into a hedge with a well-timed leap. Or a swift head-butt to the crown jewels of that smug guy at work.

Although the size of these hybrids varies depending on their lineage—maybe they're a massive son of a Standard Poodle or the petite daughter of a Miniature—they still think they're the perfect size for your lap and indeed for your side of the bed, and they'll lay over as much of your body as they can possibly manage.

Cute and cozy when they're clean, sweet smelling, and it's minus 5 outside, these dogs are less fun when they stink of eau-de-filthy-river, are scratching suspiciously like they might have fleas, and the temperature hasn't dropped below 90 for a month. The Cockapoo owner accepts that their pup will more often than not be a little grubby around the edges, though, as despite their love of putrid rivers and fetid puddles anything resembling a bath will have them employing full bounce to escape from their grip with a skill a butter-covered Charles Bronson would envy, and trying to brush their thick curls is a challenge for even those who lived through the era of 1980s perms.

Although owners tend to avoid the more outré of dogcessories—no diamanté collars or

turreted kennels for these pooches—these poodley characteristics remain a recessive gene. No one spends more on dog toys because the Cockapoo loves nothing more than to play fetch and the higher and faster the better. With a Frisbee fetish that'd shame a frat boy, if it's faster than a Roger Federer winning ace the Cockapoo is into it. This does result in numerous abandoned toys left high in trees, leading local geek communities to excitedly speculate that there's an underground treasure hunt just waiting to be cracked.

THE BORDER TERRIER

This is the best breed for small dog owners who don't really like small dogs. The Border Terrier is the furthest you can get from a yappy ankle-biter and is the favored dog of those people who generally think little pooches are a little ridiculous. The Border might be small in stature, but with their no-nonsense, no-fuss coat and big personality they're perfect for anyone who wants a "real dog", but doesn't have a two-acre garden. With a bark that belies her size, many's the terrified potential intruder and/or guest who's been scared into submission by her gruff staccato, only to feel a little foolish once the door opens and a creature reaching only up to mid-shin appears.

Having the appearance of a grizzly old man (or woman—facial hair gets us all in the end) from the day they open their eyes, Borders' venerable looks mean they are nearly always given Grandpa and Grandma names—think Reg, Stanley, Peggy, or Vera. And much like grandparents, they fall into two distinct camps:

THE MELLOW, LAID-BACK RETIREE

This type of Border is your grandparent who is generally happy with their lot in life. Hell, they might even be enjoying some recreational highs from the 19 types of prescription meds they're currently taking. The Border still likes a brisk walk—especially to work up an appetite as she is highly motivated by the promise of titbits—but she is equally as fond of a snooze on the sofa. The laid-back Border is, however, fiercely companionable and will follow you from room to room just to "check" on what's going on. And if anyone seriously crosses her or her loved ones, there will be hell to pay.

THE ESCAPOLOGIST

Like your elderly relative forever trying to jump out of a hospital bed/do a moonlit flit from the retirement home, the escapologist Border is energetic and full of vigor. She loves to explore and will frequently be found stuck behind sofas/halfway down rabbit holes/trapped between some bars. This means her owner needs one of two things: multiple pairs of eyes or a very good extending leash. The latter is also useful for partially containing the escapologist. A Border's other favorite trait is that of over-affection. Delightful for dog lovers, the kissy nature of this breed can be a little too intimate for those who are less canine-friendly.

Both types of Borders tend to be united on one thing—their hunting roots rarely endear them to cats, and whereas you may have acclimatized yours to the family puss, should a strange feline set foot in their garden, they will be seen off faster than a Krispy Kreme at a Weight Watchers' meeting.

THE MUTT

When is a mutt not a mutt? When it's a $1,000 "crossbreed" of course. True mutt owners know that the likes of a Basschund, Cock-a-Mo, or Zuchon don't count. (Yes, these are all real crosses—American Eskimo with Cocker Spaniel, Basset with Dachshund, and Bichon Frise with Shih Tzu.) A true mutt needs to have more unique threads of DNA in him than the bed sheets of a pay-by-the-hour motel.

A favorite pastime of mutt owners is to try to guess the lineage of their pet—those whiskers would suggest there's definitely some Schnauzer in him. A dash of ginger in a certain light and could his grandmother have been a wayward Corgi? And those disproportionately long legs definitely point to some Greyhound. Of course, the owners could find out once and for all with a DNA test, but where's the fun in that?

The mutt owners themselves vary from right-on types who rail against the elite breeds of the pedigree world to the accidental owners who couldn't say no when the neighbor's dog had puppies.

By their very nature the looks of a mutt can vary wildly, but among the mutt-owning community, and unlike anywhere else in the world, ugliness is king. Whereas parents of unfortunate-looking babies seem oblivious to their offspring's sticking-out ears or oddly spaced eyes, owners of the less-than-beautiful mutts are fully aware of their pet's esthetic shortcomings and love him more for it. Fewer teeth than legs (even if they don't have the full complement of limbs in the first place) and bald spots that'd make even Prince William reach for the clippers are as valued in a mutt as a post-1990 birth certificate is valued in Madonna's boyfriends. And a mutt's lack of photogenic-ness is no barrier to a significant social media presence, where the dog has all but taken over every single one of his owner's feeds, flashing a toothless grin and wagging his stumpy tail on a daily basis.

Is the mutt grateful for all this adoration? Is he, hell. The mutt's cheeky, care-not attitude is as much part of him as his indefinable parentage. He will inevitably be full of quirks, from a psychopathic yet completely inexplicable hatred of one particular dog in the park (usually one five times his size) to a fear of butterflies, these traits will be lovingly explained away by his indulgent owner as arising from his anonymous genealogy.

That's not to say the mutt is spoilt, though. The sensible owner's attitude of not needing a breed with a pedigree that places it 37th in line to the throne, or not paying two months' rent for a designer pup when there's plenty that need homes for free, carries through to everyday life with their mutt. That means specialist feather beds and organic shampoos make way for hand-me-down blankets and a squirt of whatever shower gel was 2-4-1 that week. Having said that, the mutt will still be allowed the occasional specially prepared chicken breast and given permission to sleep on the bed if he's been feeling a little off.

THE GERMAN SHEPHERD

GS owners are brave souls, not because of anything to do with their dog but because so many people think the breed, beloved of the police force and private security, is gonna gnaw their face off. True the GS could if she wanted to, but when there's so many more interesting things to be done, why the hell would she bother? The only thing these dogs want to guard 99 percent of the time is their back lawn of pesky cats. Oh, and their toys. Like the only child at kindergarten who's never had to let anyone else have a ride on his scooter, the GS guards her possessions with pride. Toy stealers, you have been warned.

The GS's cuteness as a puppy is woefully overlooked when the little bundles of fluff could give even the most photogenic of Andrex puppies a bottom-wiggling, clumsy-pawed run for their money.

Ferociously smart, the German Shepherd's thuggish rep doesn't take into account the intelligence of the breed. And owners, if they are unused to their pup's wily ways, may be frequently outsmarted. Basically this is not a pet for simpletons.

Incredibly loyal, look after a GS and she'll protect you against everything from armed intruders to someone trying to steal your fave spot on the sofa. She will also try to communicate with you frequently—even if your uneducated neighbors think all that whining and howling is just a racket, you know better.

Owners frequently present with exaggerated biceps. Because of all the pulling at the leash one might presume? But no. It's cos of all the vacuuming. It's a way of life for this owner, for few breeds shed more, and in mere weeks a GS can lose enough fur to clothe at least three oligarchs' wives. Picking carpets and soft furnishings that tone with the shade of your dog's fur is not the most ridiculous idea in the world, and one that every owner must have considered when doing their third vacuum clean of the day.

THE LABRADOR

Red chinos? An above-average interest in the British monarchy or the Kennedy dynasty? A very well used four-wheel drive car? Carpets older than the statehood of Alaska? A wine cellar that's worth more than a one-bedroom apartment? If you've answered "yes" to two or more of these, chances are you've got a Labrador, and chances are that your Lab is black.

One of the poshest of the breeds (possibly due to the cash it takes to quench the hunger of this gluttonous pedigree, but more on that later), the Lab is a regal dog and the perfect country companion for any wannabe lords and ladies of the manor (even if by manor you mean modest house in the suburbs).

Also known as the picnic pincher, summertime walks with a Labrador are fraught with danger. This dog invariably suffers from selective hearing, which means your shouts and screams for him to put down that sandwich/slice of cake/four-year-old child with a sandwich/slice of cake in her hand will go unnoticed, but the rustle of a wrapper signifying the opening of a sandwich will be heard two fields away.

Labs adore eating and they're not fussy. In fact, often the more disgusting and putrid the food is the better. Woe betide the owner whose Lab finds the aftermath of a makeshift toilet in a hedge used by a hiker caught short (yes, it's as disgusting as it sounds). This means the Lab owner needs to be a strict master or mistress to avoid the barrel-on-legs effect frequently suffered by the Lab who is allowed to indulge his passion for overindulgence. Well, 90 percent of the time... A dog has still got to have the occasional treat, and when he looks at you with those chocolatey eyes, those leftover sausages will be handed over and disappear quicker than you can say canine obesity.

Second only to stuffing their face, Labs adore to swim. And their requirements of water are similar to that of their food consumption—the more putrid the better. Streams that consist more of slime than water are their particular fave and they're often the ring leader of the group, kindly showing other wimpier breeds just how to jump in at the right angle to cause maximum splash.

But what the black Lab loves more than anything else is his owner. Emotionally intelligent (you may notice him hiding under the table during a family argument), fiercely loyal, and seemingly able to tell the time, the Lab will know exactly when each member of the household is expected home (well, his favorite ones, at least) and wait patiently by the door or window for that first glimpse. Absolutely nothing to do with the fact he might get the leftovers from that day's packed lunch... Nothing at all.

THE
CHIHUAHUA

Pound for pound one of the most entertaining dog breeds out there, what the Chihuahua lacks in size she makes up for in personality. Now stereotypes say the Chihuahua (this doesn't get any easier to remember how to spell, no matter how many times you type it, by the way) owner is female, dressed head to toe in pink, spends more on jewelry for her Chi (bored of typing it already) than you do your rent, and has an entire collection of special bags for her pooch to be beautifully transported in. So far, so Elle Woods. (If you don't know who Elle Woods is you're probably not even allowed to own a Chihuahua. She's the main character from *Legally Blonde* in case you really spent all of 2001 in a coma.)

Yes, there is a little truth in the stereotype—owners tend to be image conscious, a little "precious" (can you imagine them picking up the poop of a Great Dane for example? They've chosen a pet the size of other dogs, ahem, outgoings to minimize the ick factor), and the toting them round in a bag thing is really more of a necessity—are legs that size really capable of walking miles? And it's not as if you can shove a little Chi into a supermarket plastic bag...

Chihuahuas might attract high-maintenance owners, but there is no one more high-maintenance than the Chihuahua itself (it's bloody name alone conveys that). Trickier than toilet-training a toddler with a potty phobia, it's not unusual for a three-year-old Chihuahua to still leave little "presents" indoors. And when she does deign to go outside, she'll choose the most inopportune moment to squat down—a hot guy or girl walking past normally sends a direct message to her bowels to instantly evacuate in the most embarrassing way for her owner.

So Chihuahuas are fussy about where they go to the bathroom, but they're also terribly choosy about what they eat (their diet is definitely better and more expensive than their owner's) and as for the company they keep? Well it's easier to get into Berlin's notorious Berghain nightclub than to get one to like you, and that goes for whether you're a fellow canine or a human. Chihuahuas can smell neediness, so to start the bonding process you need to treat them like your new Tinder match—a little cool, a little aloof, don't give too much away, and let them come to you. Chances are this probably still won't work, but it's your best bet.

One thing they aren't picky about is who they pick a fight with and like the 5-foot nothing drunk guy taking on the entire soccer team, the Chihuahua won't back down for anyone. That Great Dane that deigned (excuse the pun) to get in their sunlight will be subjected to a barrage of barking that you know if you could translate would be frankly unprintable. Same for the Rottweiler whose head alone is three times the size of darling little Tinkerbell/Rocky (for the owner who is a fan of irony). So being an owner can feel a little like being a security guard for a member of the world's worst boy band. But when you're the only person in the world they don't hate... it's all worth it.

THE POODLE

Say Poodle and most people will think of those with a Marie Antoinette pompadour on their head and ankle grooming resembling very jazzy leg warmers, cantering in a showboat fashion along a boulevard while their owner, a skinny Frenchwoman dressed all in black, smokes a Gauloise.

And, yes, should you choose to have your Poodle groomed in this fashion, that will give a certain air of *je ne sais quoi* (literally... I don't know what the hell this thing is on the top of my head? Why are you insisting on making me look like an 80s soft rock singer? Give me some dignity) but the majority of owners (who aren't skinny, chain-smoking Parisian women) choose to clip their pooches all over, leading to far less mockery

in the doggy playground. That doesn't mean there's not a teeny yearning for a totally over-the-top show dog. For a Poodle owner, by the very nature of choosing to become one, is fond of fancies and fripperies and if their other half/conscience/time frame allowed it, they might just wish for a day or two of their beloved pet having the full fancy makeover. Shhh, we know it's a secret fantasy, we won't tell anyone if you don't...

Maybe because of this image of a fluffy bouffant head and feet, people tend to presume the Poodle is a fussy little thing who wants to lay on silk pillows all day being hand-fed delicious morsels and having its claws painted shell pink. Now as nice a life as that may sound, there's rather more to the Poodle than that. Ignore their literally "fluffy" image, like the "dumb" blonde who pretended she couldn't play pool before hustling you out of a week's wages, these dogs are deceptively clever and will outsmart anyone who thinks of them as cute and ditzy.

It's their intelligence rather than their perceived fussiness that means you have to work hard for a Poodle's affections. Seemingly unlikely but incredibly effective guard dogs, ain't no one getting over his threshold without his say-so. Think supermodel with a mixed martial arts sideline. Once he's decided you're okay, though, he'll want to be by your side a lot. Poodle owners know that their pups don't like to be left alone and that should they be foolish enough to try it there'll be hell to pay when the separation anxiety kicks in. This is where the shades of neuroticism that everyone expects from the Poodle can kick in—they simply cannot understand why you would want to leave them and, as such, complicated rituals of radios left on, doors left just so, and endless popping home to check on them are second nature to Poodle owners.

Oh and as for kids? Well this literal top dog frequently cannot see the point of them. Your Poodle thinks he is the most important thing in your life, after all, and this attention-seeking mini person shouldn't even think about trying to steal any of the limelight. Best to offer a 16-and-over door policy to keep your pooch happy.

THE DACHSHUND

Stubborn, scrappy, and noisy, if short man syndrome exists for dogs, the Dachsie is the prime example. Frequently owned by those that secretly kinda want a teeny tiny Paris Hilton pooch to pop (and possibly poop) out of a bag, but realize a dog that actually gets its paws on the ground sometimes is a lot more fun.

The petite-limbed Dachshund is invariably spoiled rotten. With no concept of her diminutive size, the Dachshund knows she rules the roost. First-time owners may have been under the misapprehension that they would be the boss of this mini beast, but a week or two in and it all becomes apparent. With all the attitude of a teenager who's worked out how to skip the porn firewall their parent took hours to set up, the Dachsie wraps her owners around her little fingers (well, little legs is probably more apt) in no time.

A great communicator, the Dachshund loves to bark, at her own reflection, garbage cans, something she doesn't like on TV, a slightly different brand of dog food, pretty much anything, and she will not be silenced by any amount of bribes. Too haughty to lower herself to obey for the promise of food, if she is not in the mood, she'll turn her head from the treatiest of the titbits, side-eyeing your embarrassing attempts to win her over.

If she is upset, her whine could be used to extract information from a military prisoner—a high-pitched cry that makes her owner feel terribly guilty. It's often just a protest that she hasn't been lifted onto the nearest cozy surface she wishes to make her bed. It's only when trying to reach anything over five inches high that this pooch realizes her size limitations; the rest of the time she considers herself a giant.

It's likely the Dachsie is some distant relative of the mole, such is her love for burrowing. She will never sit on top of anything that could be got under and woe betide the owner who leaves a clean basket of laundry on the floor post muddy walk (it's also a good idea to check your laundry pre-washing machine should you find your pooch has gone AWOL).

If it's a photogenic dog you're after, then the Dachsie is one of the best, knowing exactly how to pose and pout for the camera, with none of the dopey tongue out, lollopy head of the larger breeds. It's this natural beauty that makes them such popular dogs to feature on everything from cashmere jumpers to novelty toilet brush holders and, as such, the owner of a Dachshund is terribly easy to buy for. Just don't take your kids round when you drop off the gift because the under-5s and their clumsy ways and shortness (the Dachsie is a massive hypocrite) are generally unwanted visitors by this particular pup.

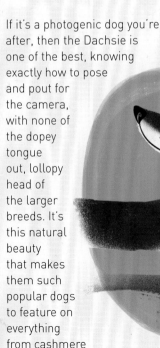

THE SHIH TZU

Let's get all our laughs out about the name right now and if you're still finding it funny, then I hope to God you never meet one crossed with a Poodle—yes, they're called exactly what you're thinking. Now the little Shih Tzu has a very long memory, as after being bred to be companions to royal families in China during the Ming dynasty they have retained that air of regality centuries later.

One of the least yappy of the toy dog breeds, Shih Tzus are affectionate and snuggly but, hand in hand with their monarchly ways, they can at times be a little princessy.

Hard floors (a shame, because the fluffy coat of the Shih Tzu makes for a rather convenient makeshift duster) and uncomfortable surfaces are no friend of the Shih Tzu who will ideally be seated on a lap at all times—the more generous in size the lap, the better. Skinny people will not impress a Shih Tzu because comfort is paramount.

The owner of a Shih Tzu tends to have the same sofa adoration as their pet companion and has definitely had many a favorite TV show ruined by the snuffles and snores of their Shih Tzu (they've since learnt to turn on the subtitles).

For most Shih Tzu lovers, the adorable snorts and snuffles of their slumbering animal become considerably less cute when it's three in the morning and they've been kept awake by the heavy breathing of the companion at the foot of their bed. New owners of Shih Tzus might want to think long and hard before they let these dogs into the bedroom at night.

In addition to the eternal quest for a comfy spot to rest her backside, the Shih Tzu is a sensitive soul when it comes to environment. Like the Goldilocks of the dog world, she doesn't like it to be too hot and she doesn't like it to be too cold—temperatures have to be just right. This means careful planning is required to achieve a Shih Tzu's optimum temperature, particularly when the mercury is creeping up on the thermometer. Hot cars/rooms/days/countries will require cooling as the Shih Tzu's short face and bountiful canine moustache, although so cute to look at, can make it a little tricky for her to breathe in the heat. Which takes us back to the Chinese royal familial origins, as you find yourself fanning a regal Shih Tzu to ensure she is at the perfect temperature.

THE PUG

With their funny little faces adorning more merchandise than that annoying "Keep Calm and Carry On" slogan, Pugs and Pug-based hashtags (#pugsnotdrugs/#puglife/#keepcalmandhugapug... ARGH, it's here too) have taken over the Internet, the world, and that sketchy knock-off shop at the back of the shopping mall that unlocks phones and sells iPooed T-shirts.

So, with specialist Pug portrait painters, dedicated Pug clothes designers, and "Pugs only" tables at restaurants (surely only a matter of time), how did the Pug get so popular? Let's break it down...

1. Pugs are like a big dog in a small body

The Pug has no concept of its size. Now, this isn't that unusual in smaller breeds but the Pug takes it to the next level. All the personality of a much bigger dog nicely wrapped up in a body that will definitely fit okay in your apartment, even if it did look much bigger when you looked round it. And yes, your husband was right that the sofa would make the room look much smaller, but that's not for now.

2. They are hilarious

The pug owner could probably chuck out their TV for a week (yes, we know everyone watches everything online now, but you know what we mean) and wouldn't even notice, because these dogs are little limelight-loving attention hoggers who simply love to show off. Clever and funny, they love being the center of attention, even if you are just laughing at their decibel-defying snoring.

3. They are cute

Kind of like the supermodel with the gap in her teeth, a Pug's pretty/ugly looks have the breed aficionados hooked. Named after an old word for goblin, their squishy, bug-eyed looks are strangely adorable.

Plus they're mega photogenic, particularly when you've put them in a hilarious Halloween/Christmas/Easter/premiere of the new Marvel movie outfit. Every Pug owner has an album on their phone specifically dedicated to their pooch.

4. They have royal heritage

With a heritage that began on the laps of Chinese emperors, where they were watched over by armed guards, it's no surprise that the Pug's aristocratic ways can attract the slightly more "princess" type of owner (don't panic—rumors that the Pug has become "basic" are largely exaggerated). Queen Victoria had a whopping 36 of them and the Duke of Windsor was so devoted to his that when he passed away one dog died himself of a "broken heart." SOB!

5. They are sensitive

Most dogs can sense when you're upset, but a Pug is so attuned to its owner's feelings it's like she's been given the password to your iPhone.

6. They are great couch potato companions

No one is saying Pug owners are lazy. Carrying those little lumps around when they decide they've snuffled enough under their own steam for the day is hard work, but after a little 20-minute daily trot—okay, 10 minutes if it's warm—they're pretty happy to pitch up on the couch and snore their way through a not inconsiderable amount of Netflix. Dreamy.

INDEX